# Be Different, Dare to Be

## by Helen Simpson Orcutt

Every night before we go to bed,

my Momma looks to me.

With wonder in her eyes she says,

be different, dare to be.

My brain is something special,

she tells me every night.

There is no need to be someone else,

when who I am is just right.

In our home we celebrate our differences,

we celebrate who we are.

Everyone is unique,

everyone is their own bright star.

I used to get upset.

I used to get mad at my quirks.

My Momma told me to stop,

because being different has its perks.

Sometimes when I touch things,

they don't feel like they should.

They send my brain into panic,

they just don't feel so good.

But I can also sing,

and I paint the prettiest flowers.

My friends love when I make them things,

I can paint for hours.

Sometimes I can't focus on m
school work or at home,

and I need to be redirected.

Sometimes I get flustered bu
teachers and friends help me,

I never get neglected.

But I can also read really well, better than most kids in my class.

We all have things we're good at,

and those are just the facts.

Sometimes I need help learning,

new things in different ways.

You might understand it,

but I need to be shown it for several days.

But I can make you laugh,

and I can make you smile.

I have lots of funny jokes,

that will keep us laughing for awhile.

Every night before we go to bed,

my Momma looks to me.

With wonder in her eyes she says,

be different, dare to be.

Sometimes I do things without thinking,

that get me in a mess.

I make some big and little mistakes,

and cause myself some stress.

But I am really brave,

and I am not afraid of much.

My friends and family always tell me,

I am super tough!

Sometimes I get picked on,

Because I am smaller than most my age.

I don't grow fast and I get sick a lot,

I hope it's just a stage.

But I have a heart of gold,

and I am a really, really good friend.

If you are hurting, sad or lonely,

I can help you mend.

Sometimes I go to special classes,

that help me with my speech.

Words can be really tricky,

so they help me practice each.

But I can run really fast,

and I can beat you in a race.

I will run so fast you won't catch me,

like a rocket into space!

Every night before we go to
bed,

my Momma looks to me.

With wonder in her eyes she
says,

be different, dare to be.

Sometimes I get angry,

and don't want to be around anyone.

Sometimes I get really crabby,

and I'm not a lot of fun.

But I can say I'm sorry,

and I can change my attitude.

I can turn around my day with help,

and be in a better mood.

Sometimes it's really hard for me

to read a clock or tell the time.

My Momma lets me wear a special watch,

and we practice at supper time.

My brain may work different,

but I am still the best version
of me.

We are all different,

and it's okay to be!

I know as I get older,

that things will start to get
harder.

I'll find new quirks in who I
am,

and I will have to push
farther.

But I will also still remember

all the times I heard my
Momma say,

Be different, dare to be, my
love,

be different in your own way.

From the Author -

My brain is different, too, just like you! It's a beautiful brain that marches to its own drum! Each day I hope you celebrate your brain and what makes you different. Why? Because what makes you different, makes you beautiful. Don't ever, ever forget that, little one.

Love, Helen

Made in the USA
Monee, IL
01 September 2019

NO TWO BRAINS ARE
THE SAME.

READ ALONG WHILE
WE CELEBRATE OUR
GIFTS AND OUR
DIFFERENCES.

ISBN 9781792901225

90000

9 781792 901225